# FINDING A SPIRITUAL COMMUNITY

# FINDING A SPIRITUAL COMMUNITY

## COMPANIONS FOR THE JOURNEY

PEG THOMPSON

HAZELDEN®

Hazelden Educational Materials
Center City, Minnesota 55012-0176

©1994 by Peg Thompson
All rights reserved. Published 1994
From *Finding Your Own Spiritual Path: An Everyday Guidebook* © 1994 by Peg Thompson,
published by Hazelden Foundation, October 1994.
Printed in the United States of America
ISBN: 1-56838-007-0

*Editor's note*
Hazelden Educational materials offers a variety of information on chemical dependency and related areas. Our publications do not necessarily represent Hazelden's programs, nor do they officially speak for any Twelve Step organization.

The people in the stories that appear in this booklet are composites of many individuals. Any resemblance to any one person, living or dead, is strictly coincidental.

Acquisitions Editor: Judith Delaney
Manuscript Editor: Debora O'Donnell Tavolier
Cover design/Interior design: David Spohn
Copywriter: Alex Acker
Typesetter: Universal Press & Link, Minneapolis, Minnesota
Production Editor: Cynthia Madsen
Print Manager: Joan Seim
Printer: Rose Printing, Tallahassee, Florida
Managing Editor: Donald H. Freeman
The typeface used in this booklet is Adobe Garamond

*When you see geese heading south for the winter flying in a "V" formation, you might be interested in knowing...why they fly that way. As each bird flaps its wings, it creates an uplift for the bird immediately following it.... Whenever a goose falls out of formation, it suddenly feels the drag...of trying to do it alone, and quickly gets back into formation to take advantage of the lifting power of the bird immediately in front of it....*

*When the lead goose gets tired, it rotates back in the wing and another goose flies at the point....The geese honk from behind to encourage those up front to keep up their speed.** *

For whatever reason, many of us have learned to get by without relying on other people, by generally fending for ourselves. Thus, we do not trust that others could nurture or support us. We don't know how to ask for what we need from others. Spiritually, we grow as best we can on our own. We may read books about spirituality, try out prayer

---

\* Author unknown.

practices, or attend seminars or workshops.

We might avoid making any true connection with a spiritual community for many years. We probably don't feel comfortable attending church or temple. If we are involved in support groups at all, we remain on the fringes. Perhaps we've been invited to join friends in rituals or on spiritual retreats but have turned them down. Maybe a traumatic experience made us believe that a solitary spiritual journey is the only safe one.

If we're people who have always covered up our feelings, we may be understandably reluctant to join a spiritual community. Being in relationship with others in our spiritual lives means that we have to overcome the ways we have survived so far—concealing our real thoughts and feelings from ourselves and others, withholding ourselves from spiritual connection with God (or the divine as we understand it).

First, we must allow what we need and hunger for, and what we fear, to come to the surface. Although inner promptings can give us information to guide our search, they may also stir up pain and disappointment from the past—and often despair about the future. We may not know what we can expect from a spiritual community, or we may feel ashamed for not needing something from others.

At some point in our spiritual growth, though, most of us find that traveling alone feels restrictive rather than safe. It can be difficult to sustain prayer practices on our own. We may be surprised to find ourselves envious of friends who have found companionship in a spiritual community. Deep inside, we realize that our spirit needs constant nourishment and guidance.

This dawning awareness nudges us out of our isolation and toward self-knowledge and self-disclosure. Everyone feels the inner prompting in his or her own time and way. If we honor our feelings, longings, and questions, we will have a sense of clarity as we search for a spiritual community.

## SEARCHING FOR A COMMUNITY

My search for a spiritual community may help you to follow your authentic path, whatever it may be. Notice and value your emotional and intellectual reactions—positive and negative—as you read on. They are windows into your inner world.

I was raised in a liberal Protestant church. An innately religious and spiritual child, I loved the music I heard during Sunday services. I was engaged by the stories and ideas I heard there. Ours was a warm community, one that welcomed children. Our minister emphasized the loving and compassionate side of Christianity. Our community valued diversity of belief and stressed respect for each individual's unique way of understanding God. As was the tradition in our church, worship was very simple and spare, focusing primarily on the verbal aspect of faith rather than on Communion. My experiences in this church gave me both the freedom to follow the promptings of my spirit and an interest in others' journeys.

As a teenager, I felt a gnawing hunger, a longing I could not even begin to articulate. My intense curiosity led me to visit a number of churches and synagogues and to read about many religious traditions. In retrospect, I understand that I was looking for a more sensuous, more ritual-centered, and probably more ancient form of worship—one that could touch me more symbolically and internally, more through feelings and senses than through the intellect.

When I was nineteen, I joined a different church. The liturgy (and, really, only that) had attracted me. I knew that I did not "believe in" many of the teachings of that church, but its Communion ritual moved me deeply. Through it I felt simultaneously connected with the earth, humanity, and God. I felt a spiritual kinship with the millions of others who have adhered to this tradition throughout the ages.

In my twenties, I began to believe that women were oppressed, both by our society and by the church. I began to think of myself as a feminist. My life in the church community was colliding with my relationships in the feminist community. Though my parish bent over backward to affirm women, the church as an institution seemed more and more inhospitable to my soul. Eventually, I came to believe that Christianity—not just my church—was inherently damaging to women. I rejected it and stopped attending altogether.

However, this was not to be the end of my story. I did not understand until much later, after I began attending Twelve Step meetings, that when I renounced my church, I had abandoned my soul too. In the Twelve Step program, I found fellow seekers with a set of spiritual principles who shared my struggles and accepted me without judgment. By example, the group showed me how to use these principles to reorient me to a spiritual life.

As I became more committed to prayer and meditation, I felt a deepening connection with an unnameable holy presence. In time, I felt the need to find a community of other seekers who could nurture my budding spiritual life.

I also participated in earth-centered and feminist rituals for earth holidays such as solstice. I felt a spiritual connection during those experiences, but I was frustrated by the infrequency of the ritual. At times, I even felt alienated.

I studied American Indian religions, and their beliefs and rituals touched a responsive chord deep within me. Though they are still a part of my spiritual life, I will always feel a barrier to full participation because I am not Indian.

In my early forties, I began to think about attending church again and to ask friends about their churches. Even so, when Sunday morning came, I couldn't get myself to church. One friend told me about his small and informal church, where Communion was every Sunday and sermons were delivered by members of the congregation, and invited me to come sometime.

I felt excited about the possibility of finding a community to support my spiritual life. But I was afraid too—afraid that I would somehow lose the spiritual way I felt an inner knowing about. These were my reactions, but I said only that I might come sometime.

Months later, my friend invited me to church again. I expressed my fears indirectly by saying that I didn't want to get dressed up, but he reminded me the service was informal. I said that I didn't want to get up early, but he said just to come sometime if I ever did.

I did wake up early one Sunday and went to the

service, watching like a hawk for anything that excluded women. But I found nothing to quarrel with. The minister was a woman who used many images and pronouns to refer to God. The worship was similar to my childhood church but included weekly Communion too. I had found a church that had incorporated all the best for me personally. I had needed to know that persons with a wide variety of beliefs and relationships with Jesus were welcome. I found there the tolerance and welcome I needed.

I discovered that I had changed too, becoming more open-minded, less hasty to defend my beliefs. I was now secure enough spiritually that I wasn't threatened by different beliefs. It took awhile, but eventually I went every week. I've been a member now for several years and know many wonderful people. I still take part in rituals of other communities too. I know that as I change and grow, my relationship with all my spiritual communities will continue to evolve.

You might want to think about your reactions to my story. ✍

## HOW OUR PREVIOUS EXPERIENCES AFFECT OUR SEARCH FOR COMMUNITY

Many people begin to nurture a spiritual life only to have it wilt or fade out because they can't find a community that fits for them. Often people who feel wounded by earlier experiences start the search with powerful fears, doubts, and resentments.

### FAMILY EXPERIENCES

Our family provides our first experience of community. If we learned there that belonging to a community means being terrified, we may have internalized the feeling that a community offers little of value. If we were mocked, humiliated, or sexually violated, we were trapped with nowhere to go. Joining a community may remind us of being trapped or losing ourselves.

Our background may keep us from distinguishing between harmful and healthy spiritual communities and leaders. We might not even recognize obvious problems or aberrant behavior, because it feels normal or familiar. For example, a survivor of sexual abuse may be vulnerable to sexual exploitation by a minister or someone else in a powerful position.

Sometimes a painful background sends us in the other direction: we seek the perfect spiritual community—one that consistently lives up to the ideal of love and solidarity. We may even think we have found it at times. When we see the inevitable imperfections, we may leave in disappointment or rage.

Sometimes we are particularly susceptible to a charismatic but tyrannical spiritual leader who demands unconditional allegiance. Or maybe family members cause us to feel so threatened that we can't develop a relationship with a spiritual group of people. If any of these sound familiar to you, write down how your family experiences have kept you from joining a spiritual community. We will discuss what you can do to change this later. ✍

### OUR EXPERIENCES WITH CHILDHOOD RELIGIOUS COMMUNITIES

Childhood religious communities often teach us what we should expect from a community. Many people found their church or temple to be a sustaining force that softened the impact of bad childhood experiences or the pain of abuse and neglect.

A woman relates here how her church experiences gave her predictability and self-worth, which counteracted the chaos she lived with at home:

> The church I attended had lots of ritual, and the ritual was very meaningful to me. Things would be done the same way every time. I could count on it. There was a group of people who understood the mystery of ritual, how it used visible objects to point to invisible realities. That captured my imagination. During services, I always felt that I belonged there, in that place with those people.
>
> In the youth group, I was able to take part in services, speak, and lead prayer. I felt that I was just as good as anyone else when it came to communicating with God.

One man describes the sense of belonging he got from the church he attended as an adolescent:

> When I was about seventeen, I started going to the Disciples of Christ church in town. When I joined the church, there was a strong sense of family. That was important. I loved the sense of brotherhood that I found in the church. People called each other Brother So-and-So and Sister So-and-So. I loved what that symbolized—the brotherhood of humanity. It was a tremendous sense of connection.

Sometimes a religious community aggravated the wounds we received at home. If this describes you, you might have a somewhat rockier path to community. Your church might have stressed judgment or punishment, creating a climate of terror. It may have given you rigid rules about personal conduct that were impossible to understand, let alone follow. If you were raised in a religious community that didn't address the needs and abilities of children, you probably concealed or denied your feelings in order to fit in. Perhaps persons of other faiths were seen as dangerous or sinful. The daughter of an evangelical minister tells what she learned as a child:

> The message was clear: Your close relationships should be with the saved rather than the unconverted. Because they are of the world and we are not of the world, we are the chosen, we are the special, the converted—we're God's chosen people. Some Catholic kids lived behind us, and they were the only kids we played with outside the church group. With them we had to be careful, because, the message was, our values were different from theirs and we might be led into sin.

Out of this experience, this woman came to expect a religious community to include some people and exclude others. Later, searching for a spiritual community, she placed a high value on inclusiveness.

Some people suffer from the conflicts with their parents' interfaith marriage. Sometimes there are abrupt shifts of religion because of divorce or remarriage. A woman describes how this felt:

> My first memories of religion are of first, second, and third grade at the Catholic school and the rituals of the Catholic church. They're positive memories. I remember my First Communion and feeling very special in my white dress. I just felt kind of holy in the church. It was very positive for me. It was what I needed at that time.
>
> This is what I lost when my mother divorced and remarried: not only my father and my family as I had known it, but the church as well. I still feel a lot of anger and grief about losing that sense of specialness.

Belonging to a church can make a family's problems publicly visible, sometimes leaving children deeply ashamed. Here's a story about a man from a small southern town. His father, a community leader, had had a long-standing affair with a woman, and the two had a daughter. They all went to the only Baptist church in town. He described a typical Sunday:

> We would sit five pews up from the back, on the left side, every week. My half-sister and her mother and her grandmother sat toward the front on the right side.
>
> My anxiety in church reached its peak when it was time for someone from each family to take an offering to the altar. Every Sunday I was expected to take it my family. We all went down the center aisle to the altar and returned along the outer aisle, beginning at the front on the right side.
>
> I always became aware of my father's tension when his daughter would come by. He had a very warm and loving relationship with her. She would look at him as she came by. Sometimes if he

was sitting on the end, she would touch him on the arm. My mother would bristle. If I was sitting between them, I would feel the tension radiating out of both their bodies. This was a very strained time for me.

After the right side finished, I had to go around and deliver the offering. I could feel the eyes following me. The town was small, so everybody knew. It was like being in a spotlight. I wanted to disappear. I wanted to become invisible.

How does the church or temple of your childhood—or the lack of one—affect your spiritual life now? Make a few brief notes if you wish. ✍

ADULT EXPERIENCES OF COMMUNITY

Because families don't always prepare children to thrive in the world, young adulthhod was a perilous time for most people. Any unhealed wounds from childhood can affect every area of our lives—work, relationships, and the spiritual.

Many of us were lost souls as young adults.

Without knowing it, we were extremely vulnerable. Looking for a safe place to belong and attracted by a predictable environment, we may have chosen spiritual communities that weren't good for us. For example, one woman, raised in a church she enjoyed, started to question it when she became an adolescent:

> I had never been exposed to any other denomination. As a teenager, I started questioning. Why do I believe what I believe? How does what my church teaches compare with what other churches teach? I did ask my pastor and he just gave me a book to read. That didn't answer my questions; in fact, it stirred up a few more.
>
> So when I went to college, I was looking for answers. I went to some Campus Crusade for Christ meetings. At first, I got answers. I think I was looking for someone else to give me direction. The people in the Crusade readily provided that. They gave me a

clear list of what I could and couldn't do. For example, if you didn't have your quiet times and study the Bible for a half hour every day, something was really wrong with your spiritual life.

Initially, they were kind of nice. Later, they made me feel that no matter what I did, it was never enough. I lost my own sense of what was important to me because I was so indoctrinated with what was supposed to be important. It was very powerful.

For a lot of people, the spiritual journey brings us to the truth about ourselves—what we believe, who we are. For some of us, this means coming out as bisexuals, gay men, lesbians, or transgender persons. While some religious communities affirm those of all sexual orientations, others require secrecy as the price of belonging. One woman shares this story:

In the early years of our marriage, my husband and I belonged to an evangelical church. Gradually, he realized he was gay. Suddenly, our circumstances weren't suitable to talk about at church. You just knew from sermons or how the members talked about these "other [gay] people" that all of a sudden you would be one of "them." Or you'd become a missions outreach project, where the whole congregation was trying to fix you.

I really felt trapped. I knew my life needed to take another direction, but there would be heavy consequences. We lost everything when we left—all our friends, our livelihood, and our church. After we left, I had people come to me and say that I was on my way to hell because I wasn't going to church.

In exploring a specific spiritual community, we gradually become more aware of its beliefs, doctrines, and rules of conduct. We have more experience with its emotional climate, and our sense of safety may be altered for better or for worse.

Conflict may arise between our values and those of the community at any point. A seminary student received a distraught call from a young relative:

> Visiting a church of her own denomination, this young woman became upset by an unfamiliar practice and phoned me frantically. "We filled out Communion cards to register that we were taking Communion," she said in a voice full of agitation, "and below the place where you write your name and address there was a little statement that said something like 'We at Emmanuel Church believe when you take Communion you partake of the body and blood of our Lord, Jesus Christ. We also believe that the potential for harm in taking Communion is as great as its benefits, for if you take Communion without believing these things, you bring judgment upon yourself.'"
>
> Fearfully, she asked me, "Am I a sinner because all this time when I took

Communion I always believed it was a symbolic ritual? Have I really put my soul in danger?"

One woman, recovering from alcoholism, had faced the painful truth about the many ways she had hurt her children while she was drinking. When she joined a group that followed the sweat lodge practice of the Lakota tribe, her guilt made her feel unfit to participate:

I believed I shouldn't go into the sweat lodge with the others. I felt I wasn't worthy, that it was something I didn't have a right to participate in because of all the wrong things I had done in my life. Maybe I didn't want anyone to know about it. When you go into the sweat lodge, you bare your sins.

But somehow I knew that this group of people had to be part of my recovery. I had to find a way to tell them. Finally, I went back. I felt so vulnerable. I remember sobbing and sobbing. I was asking for forgiveness as a parent. People just listened. It was really healing. I had such tender feelings.

Have any of these experiences reminded you of your own? What shaped your feelings about spiritual communities? Make a brief note of them now. ✍

## WHAT WE HAVE A RIGHT TO EXPECT FROM A SPIRITUAL COMMUNITY

Despite these obstacles, as we follow a spiritual path, most of us find that we need companions. Yet past experiences might have left us unsure of what to expect and ask for from a spiritual group. Every spiritual community has imperfections. Yet for each of us, there is one that closely fits our needs and preferences and can foster our spiritual life. Not every community can accept every one of us, so it is up to us to search for or create one that can. Wherever we participate, we do have a right to feel safe. The doctrines of the spiritual community, its images of God or the sacred, and the style of relating in the community we choose should allow us to open spiritually. When we reveal information about ourselves it should be received with respect and care.

At the heart of any spiritual community are stories of humanity's relationship with the sacred. The scripture, tradition, preaching, and personal sharing of the community should resonate with our own story in a real, albeit imperfect, way. What we hear should move and touch us, allowing us to be more open with ourselves, other people, and our Higher Power.

Each of us has different spiritual needs. We may feel most connected to the sacred through conversation, scripture reading, ritual, music, silence, communal prayer, or other activities. The community we choose must offer much of what we need to thrive spiritually most of the time. This is not too much to expect.

Along with nurturing our spirit, we need challenge in order to grow spiritually. We need to learn more about ourselves, grow in our caring for ourselves and others, and examine our spiritual blocks. A spiritual community should help us with these, but not overwhelm us.

## ONE WAY TO FIND A SPIRITUAL COMMUNITY

To begin, you must accept a paradox. On one hand, you will need to sharpen your awareness through reflection, gather information, and make responsible decisions. On the other, you will need to be ready for new and unexpected experiences, not try too hard, and be ready for the right spiritual community when it comes into your life. Though you might have to do some work to find a spiritual home, it's not really going to be an achievement, but a sacred gift. Each step offers reliable guidance only when you stay open to the unexpected touch of the divine.

### REFLECTION AND PRAYER

Reflection and prayer can help you stay centered and calm as you learn more about spiritual communities. Your spiritual voice can tell you who you are as you start to look. In reflection, ask yourself: What do I need? What do I want? What is absolutely critical for me right now? What are my strengths? What do I have to offer? What do I need to guard against? Through reflection, you learn what has worked before. You can pray for guidance or enter a place of stillness within to listen for direction.

Keeping in mind the qualities that are most important to you, you may rule out some denominations, congregation sizes, or styles of worship. If you already belong to a church or other group, you can evaluate what *is* working.

As you reflect and pray, you can use writing or dialogue to honor your emerging wisdom and to remember what you learned. You can journal to follow your exploration and record the results. You can talk with someone and let this person reflect your ideas back so they are newly illuminated. You may be hesitant to speak your truth because it is fragmented, confused, or vague. But if you dare to give voice to it, you might find it offers fresh insights and opens the way to further exploration.

### GATHERING INFORMATION

When you feel you know enough about yourself,

you can gather information about different communities. One of the best ways to do this is to conduct interviews as you would if you were looking for a job. You can create questions and use them as a guide when you interview people. You may choose people in a support group, especially those you've learned from. Friends or acquaintances can tell you about their churches, synagogues, or spirituality groups. You can follow up with reading.

Unexpected opportunities may turn up for taking part in someone else's community. You might be invited to a Shabbat meal, a solstice ritual, a wedding, or a retreat. Watch yourself as you make the decision to accept or decline. If you take part, all your feelings and thoughts will give you information about your needs for community.

On your own, you might attend services at a church or synagogue, participate in a retreat, or sign up for a yoga or t'ai chi class. Maybe you could gather a few friends for an informal spirituality group. Or you might try a few meetings of a Twelve Step group.

Through the whole information-gathering

process, you can reflect and pray to gain deeper understanding of what you're learning and what it all means. If you don't like some experience, reflecting on it will sharpen your perceptions about what didn't match your needs. If you are attracted to a community, prayer may help you articulate why. You may find rich insights in unexpected reactions.

You may need months or even years to gather information. You will have your own methods and your own timetable, and you can work steadily or in spurts. There's no need to reach any quick conclusion. Everything you learn has value in guiding your future steps.

## Becoming Involved

Your search will probably lead you to a community that will attract you. As you begin a relationship with this community, you can draw on reflection, prayer, and the information-gathering skills you have now.

Participating in a spiritual or religious community is an active process that requires many decisions, big and small. You'll need to decide what and with whom to share information about yourself. You eventually will decide when to join (if at all) and how you want to act on your commitment. Since you and your chosen community will always be changing and growing, you may even need at some point to decide if you will leave. Seeking spiritual community is a lifelong process.

The Exploration and Discovery section contains three exercises, each with a different focus. Take a few minutes now to look them over and decide which one you would like to do first. When you are ready, do the Passageway exercise.

❦

## PASSAGEWAY

Take a few minutes to settle yourself. Let your body relax. When you are ready...

Imagine yourself as a plant growing in a garden. Take your time, and let the image come into your awareness on its own ❦ taking shape

28

gradually ❧ or all at once. ❧ There is no need to force it. Just allow the image to be born. ❧

As the image becomes clearer, feel your size. ❧ Are you tall or short, sturdy or delicate? Become aware of your form. ❧ Are you wispy or bushy? ❧ Be aware of your leaves ❧ their size ❧ and shape ❧ and color. ❧

Now turn your attention to your surroundings. ❧ Where are you growing? ❧ Are you in the shade ❧ or in the sun? ❧ In a large garden ❧ or a small one? ❧ Are there other plants near you? ❧ Touching you? ❧ What are they like? ❧

What time of year is it? ❧ Are you feeling the new growth of spring ❧ or the blooming time of summer ❧ or the seedtime of fall ❧ or the resting time of winter? ❧ Feel the light on your leaves and stems. ❧ Is it strong or weak? ❧ Bright or filtered? ❧ Feel the air moving around you. Is it chilly or mild? ❧ Dry or moist? ❧ Is there a breeze or a wind? ❧ Let yourself feel the air and the light around you. ❧ Now feel the soil around your roots. ❧ Is it moist or dry? ❧ Cool or warm? ❧

Let yourself experience the other creatures in the garden where you stand. ✤ Perhaps there are children playing nearby ✤ or birds singing ✤ or frogs croaking ✤ or butterflies flitting from blossom to blossom. ✤ Perhaps the gardener is tending the garden ✤ or picking flowers ✤ or harvesting vegetables. ✤ Maybe a rabbit or a mouse is nearby. ✤

Take a few minutes to rest in your awareness of yourself and your surroundings. ✤ Let the scene unfold or change ✤ or just stay the same. ✤ Allow yourself to relax in this time and place. ✤ Just rest in this spot. ✤ Now gently return to the present moment.

✤

**EXPLORATION AND DISCOVERY**

In this section you will explore in more detail your experiences with community, both religious and spiritual. Remember that you are the authority. You know when and where you have experienced community.

## EXERCISE 1:
### EXPLORING YOUR HISTORY
### WITH COMMUNITY

In your journal or on a large sheet of paper, make a list of all the religious and spiritual communities you've participated in, leaving a space after each entry. Begin with your childhood church or synagogue and work up to the present. Feel free to include even brief contacts and any communities, such as Scouts or a musical group, that fed you spiritually, whether it was explicitly religious or not.

When you've finished, take a few minutes to look it over. Mark with an asterisk (*) communities of particular importance to you—either positive or negative—in your search for a spiritual path.

Now choose one of your marked entries. Take a few minutes to remember your experiences in this community, and then write your responses to some or all of the following questions. You can work quickly or slowly, but try to be as honest as you can. Include fragments that seem important, even if you don't know exactly why.

- How was this community important to you?
- What did you learn there about what it means to belong to a religious community? Include both spoken and unspoken messages. You may want to complete this sentence in a number of ways: From this congregation or group, I learned…
- How, if at all, has your participation in this community sustained you on your spiritual path?
- How, if at all, are your present spiritual struggles related to your participation in this community?
- What, if anything, did you learn or receive there that is still valuable to you? Be as specific as you can.

Answer these questions for one or two more of your marked entries. ✍

When you've finished, you may want to take a break. When you come back, look over what you've written. Note in your journal what stands out for you. If there's anything you want to add or write more about, go ahead. ✍

## EXERCISE 2:
### Identifying the Members Of
### Your Present
### Spiritual Community

Turn to a blank page in your journal. Take a few minutes to quiet yourself.

When you are ready, ask yourself the following question: Where do I feel a sense of spiritual community now? (Remember that a spiritual community can include both people who have died and those who are living, people you've met and those you don't know.) Quickly and briefly write down everything that comes to mind. Let it flow and try not to censor yourself. Do not stop to explore or censor right now. When you reach a natural pause, ask yourself the question again and write anything else that comes up. Repeat this process until your list seems complete. ✍

Now take a short break to stretch or relax.

When you return, add to your list anything that may have occurred to you during the break. ✍

Now go back over your list. Beside each entry, describe how the person or thing increases or strengthens your relationship with your Higher Power. Take all the time you need. ✍

Take another short break. When you come back, look over everything you've written. Be aware of your feelings as you do.

### EXERCISE 3:
#### IDENTIFYING QUALITIES THAT YOU DESIRE IN A SPIRITUAL COMMUNITY

Take a few minutes to focus your attention by using the Passageway exercise or any other method that works for you. When you're ready, reflect on the qualities you're looking for in a spiritual community. In your journal, quickly jot down the qualities that occur to you. For now, try not to think too much about them; just let them flow onto the page. ✍

When you reach a natural stopping point, sit quietly for a few minutes. Note any other characteristics that come to mind.

Now, if you wish, use the list on pages 37-40 to expand your own list. Copy words that fit for you into your journal. ✍

When you feel that your list is complete, look it over for a few minutes. Which qualities are absolutely crucial to your spiritual growth and well-being? Mark them with a symbol of your choice. Which are desirable but not crucial? Mark them with another symbol. Now review your list again and fine-tune it. ✍

Take a brief break at this point to take a walk or drink a cup of tea or coffee. Stretch your body and allow your mind to wander. When you feel refreshed, look over your list. Write your answers to some or all of the following questions: ✍

• How do you feel about the work you have done on this exercise so far?

- What do the qualities you have identified have in common? How are they related? Is there a central value or idea that connects them?

- What are the conflicts or contradictions, if any, among the qualities you have listed?

- If you have participated in spiritual or religious communities in the past, which of your listed qualities, if any, did they have? Which did they lack? What were the dominant qualities of these communities?

- If you participate in one or more spiritual communities now, which qualities do they have? Which do they lack? What are the dominant qualities of these communities?

- What questions, if any, does this exercise raise for you?

Now is a good time to let what you've learned "cook" for a while.

# DESIRABLE QUALITIES
## OF SPIRITUAL COMMUNITIES

### A

accepting
accessible
active
alive
approachable
attentive
available

### B

beneficent
bold
bountiful
busy

### C

calm
captivating
caring
challenging
clergy-led
close

concerned
comforting
compassionate
complex
consistent
constant
content
courteous
creative
courageous

### D

dependable
dispassionate
dynamic

### E

ecstatic
educational
egalitarian
emotional
energetic

engaging
enthusiastic
expressive

F

fair
faithful
familiar
feminine
feminist
flexible
forgiving
forthright
fresh
friendly
fulfilling
fun

G

generous
gentle
glad
gracious

H

happy
hardworking
hierarchical
honest

I

imaginative
impartial
inclusive
independent
innovative
inspiring
intellectual
intelligent
intense
intimate
inventive
involved

J

joyful
justice-oriented

**K**

kind
knowing

**L**

large
lively
loving

**M**

masculine
maternal
mellow
musical

**N**

nearby
new
nontraditional
nurturing

**O**

objective
old

open
open to conflict
original

**P**

passionate
participatory
paternal
peaceful
persistent
playful
powerful
principled
private
protective

**Q**

questioning
quiet

**R**

rational
reassuring
receptive

refreshing
relaxed
reserved
respectful
responsive
restrained
risk-taking

S

safe
sensitive
serene
serious
service-oriented
sincere
small
simple
solid
soothing
spirited
stable
steadfast
strong

structured
supportive
sustaining
sympathetic

T

tactful
temperate
tolerant
traditional
trustworthy

V

vigorous
vital
vulnerable

W

warm
welcoming
wise

## REFLECTION AND INTEGRATION

Begin by reading everything you have written in the exercises. Note any new insights or questions that spontaneously occur to you. Then write your responses to some or all of these questions: ✍

- What patterns do you see in your history with community?

- How are your present and past experiences of community related? Are they harmonious? How? Do they clash? How?

- Have there been shifts or breaks in your choices about community? How would you describe them?

- What's missing for you now in terms of spiritual community?

- What might be your next step(s) in exploring spiritual community?

- Is there anything else you have learned about yourself and community?

## ABOUT THE AUTHOR

Peg Thompson, Ph.D., offers psychotherapy, spiritual direction, consultation, and training services through her private practice in St. Paul, Minnesota. She is the author of *Finding Your Own Spiritual Path: An Everyday Guidebook*, published by Hazelden (October 1994). She also teaches a course on religious and spiritual development at two Twin Cities graduate schools. When not working, she can often be found tending her garden or fishing in a trout stream. She lives with her partner and their two dogs in a rural setting near the Twin Cities.